IS THIS YOU?

Your personal library is filled with volumes of
Self-Help, New Age, New Thought, Old Thought,
Religious, Anonymous books.

IS *THIS* YOU?

Your personal circumstances are more often
in crisis than *free* of crisis.

IS THIS WHY?

After making an affirmation that you are lovable and
deserving, you then go about your day, upset with
others for not doing what you think they ought to do.
You snap at your spouse, yell at the kids, drive
inconsiderately in traffic,
complain,...

ARE YOU READY TO REMODEL...
YOURSELF?

Build Your Character,
Experience Your
SELF-ESTEEM

Pardon
My Dust . . .

I'm
Remodeling

Casey Chaney

Mocha Publishing Company
8475 SW Morgan Drive
Beaverton, Oregon 97005
(503) 643-7591

ISBN 0-9626403-0-1

Library of Congress Catalog Card Number: 90-91625

Printed in the United States of America

Cover design by Jan Lochridge and Berdell Moffett

Mocha Publishing Company
8475 SW Morgan Dr.
Beaverton, OR 97005
(503) 643-7591

Dedication

To Berdell & Corey

Pardon My Dust...I'm Remodeling
I like my new foundation better and I'm opening up new doors

Pardon My Dust...I'm Remodeling
And I'm building a larger life than I had before

Acknowledgements

I would like to extend my appreciation and gratitude to the following individuals:

To my partners: Trudy, Carol and John—special thanks. You knew the Master Mind had heard me when I wasn't so sure.

To my editors: Lisa Haqq—you took on the task with love, graciousness and care (and a bright red pen); Sharon Finnestad—you loved it and gave me the courage to send it to the printer (and I knew if you thought it was good, so would everyone); Thea Rhiannon—you saved me from monumental humiliation (""!!!o"op"s"!.,)".

To Douglas "Words That Heal" Bloch: You gave us your time and knowledge about publishing. Thank you.

To the graphic artist & layout artists: Jan Lochridge, Jay Fraser, Paul Fitterer, Margo Mead—your timing was terrific.

To my investors: Mom, Lisa, Sharon, Bridget, Sandra, Steve, Janne, DeAnn, Sherry, Judi, Paul, Stuart, Mariah, Marcella, Barb—we did it!

To my spiritual support: Mary—you made space for me, believed in me and showed me how to face the fear; Fran L., Sally, Bruce, Haven, Fran S., Val, Lorrie—your positive attitudes and loving support inspired me to believe in the possibility of the impossible.

To my family: Berdell—you were all of the above—you gave me the time, the love and the encouragement...you weren't afraid to say, "Change this..." (except when you wanted me to help you with dinner); Corey—you waited patiently for us to finish (even without T.V.!); Mom—you kept saying "Good for you!" even though you had no idea what I was doing; Vic & Meta—you did all the worrying for me and supported me anyway; Lisa & Sharon—there are no words...

Table of Contents

Introduction

THIS BOOK IS ABOUT TAKING ACTION—
QUALITY ACTION—actively demonstrating productive,
positive attitudes and behaviors in life as it is being lived.
It is about achieving freedom, health, happiness and prosperity in our lives by choosing thoughts, words and actions of excellence.

The consequence of mediocrity is disappointment.
There is no sense in remodeling if the materials we are

using are substandard, for when we begin living with the finished product, we will know we have cheated ourselves. If we are interested in feeling great, we must conduct ourselves with greatness. And every one of us can do that.

Practicing greatness means risking the truth when we would feel safer practicing deception; it means giving when we feel the need to withhold; it means wishing the best for those who seem to deserve the worst. It's as simple as that.

Bringing greatness into our lives requires some active remodeling. Breaking down the living room wall is frightening, but it must be risked if there is to be an expansion of living space. Are you ready for a larger life? If so, it's all about action—*QUALITY* ACTION.

I believe you are striving for greatness and excellence, just as I am, and I've written this book with that idea in mind. *Pardon My Dust...I'm Remodeling* is focused on finding and putting into action the very best within you. The result will be the emergence of a person you will love...you!

Chapter 1

Does Any Of This Sound Like You?

Your personal library is filled with volumes of Self-Help, New Age, New Thought, Old Thought, Religious, Anonymous books. You've meditated, vegetated and finally hesitated. Something's missing.

You've studied assertiveness techniques and tried to put them into practice. Either you feel terribly uncomfortable asking for what you want or you've become forceful and self-righteous about your requests. There's rarely a happy medium.

You've contemplated creative visualization and tried to apply the concepts by saturating yourself with affirmations. Few of them have become even remotely believable to you. You've tried to flood out the negative messages with more affirmations, but the messages still come up.

You want healthier people and things in your life. You want to feel comfortable and secure. You have awakened to new self-help ideas, applying the concepts with only occasional wins. Your personal circumstances are more often *in* crisis than *free* of crisis.

You have been trying to achieve a lasting sense of self-esteem but none of the methods you've used have worked. Instead, your sense of self-esteem is more like short-lived bursts of willpower. No matter how much you try to believe in yourself, you continue to suffer from doubt—doubt that you really can get what you want in your life, doubt that you have what it takes to make the right decisions, doubt that the universe really wants to give to you.

This is everyone's story. It's yours. It's mine. We are all in this together. Through our need for individual expression, we often prefer to think of ourselves as very separate from one another. The word "individual," however, means "undivided." Contrary to what many people think, we are merely individual parts of the same whole. Though our features are different and our interests and desires varied, we are alike when it comes to our basic needs. We all know what it feels like to want, to be loved, to be hurt, to be afraid. We have been able to help one another as the result of our similarities. This is the reason behind the phenomenal success of twelve-step programs such as Alcoholics Anonymous, Al-anon, Overeaters Anonymous, Co-dependents Anonymous, etc. What works for one will work for all.

Chapter 2

Remodeling

Y ou probably already know that the answer to your success lies in your decision to change yourself, not others. What to do and how to do it seems to be the dilemma.

In changing, there are two very definite steps to take. These two steps are AWARENESS and ACTION. AWARENESS simply means to open your mind to new ideas. ACTION means applying these new ideas to the things you do every day. Keep in mind that wherever there is new awareness and ensuing action, there is some degree of discomfort and conflict, otherwise known in this book as "Dust." Dust is the temporary product of changed awareness and changed actions.

On the one hand, it is very difficult to continue doing things the old way once we see things differently. On the other hand, we are creatures of habit. It isn't easy to begin doing things differently. It means stopping ourselves in the act of old thoughts and behaviors and making the change.

Our change catches those around us off guard, even though it is a change for the better. It is very much like sitting on a teeter-totter. As long as each person is the same distance from the center, no one is set off balance. But when one of the people decides to move closer to the center, becoming more balanced by themselves, the other person drops unexpectedly. They are likely to yell, "Hey! You moved. Look what you did to me." Rather than moving closer to the center themselves in order to balance you, people will often try to provoke you back to the old, destructive behaviors.

Name calling, pouting, yelling, pleading, running, lying, blaming, sarcasm—none of these methods of communication is productive. The end result is increased resentment and additional battle scars. It is up to you, at those moments, even under the pressure of habit or the disapproval of others, to remodel.

OUT WITH THE OLD

The old "stuff" has to go before the new can be applied. This "stuff" includes negative ideas, beliefs, attitudes, use of words and behaviors. There is no use in hiding the old under the new. That would be like leaving the sour milk in the pitcher and topping it off with fresh milk. All of it mixes together and the tainted milk spoils the good. We must be willing to look at the negative "stuff" we still hang on to and concede its uselessness.

This is often difficult when we are first starting out because there seems to be no direction. We are not always certain which thoughts, words and behaviors to replace.

IN WITH THE NEW

We don't have to reinvent the wheel; there are some great blueprints available to us. The blueprints are the seminars we attend, the church services, the speakers, the books, the tapes, the meetings and the classes. The blueprints are a necessary part of our remodeling for they provide us with ideas and a plan of action. But they are *not* the action itself.

Many times, when we seek a better life, we become stuck dwelling in the blueprints. It is very important to remember that the blueprints are not the action; nor are they the sensations experienced after the action. They are simply the ideas, the guides and the reminders. We use our blueprints to gain direction and measure our

progress. Without action, there is no progress to measure.

What I was failing to do was to break ground in my
daily experiences, using my blueprints. I needed to take
the mental-action of making a commitment and follow
through with it at the moment of crisis. Otherwise, I
would just enjoy the blueprints and do nothing construc-
tive with them. Then I would wonder why my life continued to repeat the same negative patterns.

In my work with others, I have found that many
people spend much of their time gathering blueprints,
expecting the monument of their life to build itself.
Seminars and tapes, special speakers and good books are
fun. Therapeutic retreats promote quiet time, relaxation,
friendships and information. That's one reason why we
enjoy the blueprints so much and indulge in them, sometimes incessantly. But when the speaker leaves the po-
dium, the seminar is over. The tape is only 90 minutes
long and every book has a back cover. The weekend is
over on Sunday evening and it's back to real life on
Monday morning. If we want to experience healing,
permanently, we need to apply the blueprints to Monday morning.

Too often, our willingness to act dissipates when we
become angry, hurt and self-righteous. Rather than
remodel our attitudes, we end up blaming our negative
choices on other people and situations. Then we go back
to our blueprints to find our temporary serenity. Or we
go looking for a new set of blueprints, having taken no

action on the ones we already have.

HEALING HAPPENS AS THE RESULT OF THE SENSATIONS WE EXPERIENCE AFTER WE HAVE TAKEN DIRECT ACTION. This means catching ourselves in the act by assessing and replacing our thoughts and reactions toward people, places and things *at the moment they are happening*. Afterward, we experience the healing feeling, and this is when our lives begin to change.

Chapter 3

Pardon My Dust

Adjusting my usual responses to life's various encounters created for me a new set of experiences. Some of the consequences of my new decisions were temporarily uncomfortable—for me and often times for those around me. As I mentioned before, I call that discomfort "Dust."

If you have ever remodeled a room or a home or watched someone else in the process, you have seen the initial Dust. Dust is the temporary residue that is created when any kind of change takes place. Where there is no Dust, there has been no action, no remodeling, and ultimately no change. When we make the decision to change our actions and reactions, there is plenty of Dust.

Suddenly caught off guard, people don't know how to respond, at least for the moment. Our new choices sometimes threaten those around us. We may be making decisions for ourselves that they would like to make also, but they don't have enough faith, courage or inspiration to take action at this time. Or perhaps they think we are taking foolish chances and they are simply worried about us. Reacting from fear, they attack our belief in possibility because they are encumbered within their own beliefs of impossibility.

This Dust can be quite irritating. First of all, we want others to accept us as we are and we want them to offer us positive support. When they don't react with enthusiasm over our decisions, we feel hurt. Second, it's scary taking risks in order to live the way we ideally choose.

We don't intend to create Dust; it just comes naturally. It is the direct result of breaking down walls, tearing out old foundation and replacing the cupboards.

Without action, without taking the risk, without experiencing Dust, there will be no chance for betterment. I remember very well the feelings I had as I walked away from my classroom on the day I resigned from teaching in order to start my own business. I felt as if I was doing the right thing, and at the same time, I was afraid of starvation and living on the streets. This would be the worst thing that could happen to me. The worst never happened. I have since learned that it rarely does. If I hadn't risked the worst, I would have missed the miracles that have manifested in my life since.

Chapter 4

Doubt

One particle of Dust is Doubt. Doubt occurs as the result of the belief that we are not good enough, not smart enough, not deserving enough, not lucky enough or just plain *not* enough.

I know a man who is incredibly creative and talented. He is an author, an actor, a poet, a teacher and a lecturer. He has not been able to bring one of his creations to a successful completion in at least fifteen years. He stops before he has promoted his projects fully. The result is that they go on the shelf until he gets a burst of willpower to try again. Just as he is beginning to get it off the ground, something inside him says "What's the use?" He begins to doubt himself.

Most people agree that self-esteem is the answer to doubt. Once a sense of self-esteem is established, we begin to believe that our goals and dreams are possible. How to establish this sense of self-esteem has been the focus of every parent, teacher, psychologist, psychiatrist, philosopher and minister, ad infinitum. So far, there have been all kinds of complex theories and books written on the subject. Yet, seeking self-esteem still seems to be our national pastime. Is there no answer?

I find it highly unlikely that the Power which created such a well-ordered universe would leave the human race in such a tentative quandary! I believe the answer to attaining a sense of self-esteem is much simpler and in order to understand and use it, we must be aware of the true nature of self-esteem.

Chapter 5

Self-Esteem

Self-esteem is a much simpler concept than most of the world seems to believe. We have made it into some elusive pot of gold. We are told that without it, we will get nowhere in life. Because of this, people are forever concerning themselves with where it comes from, how to get it and why it leaves us. Are you prepared to accept a new idea about self-esteem? It will change your life. It changed mine.

You are born with self-esteem. Without it, you could not exist. It is a natural part of you, the very core of who you are. You cannot get self-esteem nor can you lose self-esteem. It is never low nor high. It never changes. No one can take away or destroy your self-esteem, nor can they change its size or cover it up. It only seems that way at times.

This may be difficult to understand because, from the standpoint of how we feel from one moment to the next, it seems to change. But in reality, it is our perspective of life that changes, not self-esteem.

You might compare self-esteem to the sun. Depending upon Earth's particular perspective, we either see the sun or we don't, but it is still there, shining just as brightly as ever, *sustaining us*, whether we can see it at a particular moment or not. We don't blame the other planets for taking the sun away when it gets dark. We understand that it is Earth itself that turns away from the sun, and yet it is still always facing the sun from another perspective. When we are on the side facing away from the sun, things appear dark, even though these things have not changed color, size or shape at all.

This is how it is with self-esteem. *We turn away from it ourselves* by what we choose to think, say and do, yet our self-esteem is still with us in full. We simply have no sense of it. We alone place a veil of mental pollution between ourselves and our self-esteem with our own negative thoughts, our own negative words and our own negative behaviors, blinding ourselves to our highest potential.

The talented man who was mentioned in the previous chapter suffers from some very negative attitudes toward people and circumstances. His choice of thoughts is very often laced with blame, self-righteousness, doom-and-gloom and anger. This comes out through his words: "Another screw-up!" and "That jackass!" and "I can't afford..." and "With my luck...." His behavior, which is studded with routine temper tantrums and deep depression, is another indication of the fact that his thinking is quite negative. Self-doubt sets in and then, ultimately, the attitude of "What's the use?" Another promising creation gets shelved.

He unconsciously turns away from his own self-esteem. He is completely unaware that he has choices (choices to look for the good, choices of positive talk, choices of positive perceptions and attitudes), which would clear the air for him to see his self-esteem, to see that he could succeed. Instead, he listens only to his fears and insecurities and acts on them, blaming matters outside himself for his thoughts and behaviors. His negative thoughts and behaviors create for him embarrassment, shame and self-hatred—the pollution is so thick that he swears he hasn't got whatever it takes to be successful. He just can't see it.

Not everyone is as extreme an example as this man. Perhaps you, too, want something special but you don't believe it is possible to attain. Perhaps you, too, have a strong desire or dream for your life, yet something inside you is convinced you will never see it happen. This doubt is caused by your own negative thinking and behaviors. You may be completely oblivious to what these are. They may not even appear as negative at this time. I invite you to keep an open mind as to what these may be.

We have blamed others for our own inability to experience our self-esteem and have often spent years attempting to get back that which was never taken away. Regardless of what others may have thought, said or done to us, it was always our own perspective of those incidents that created our pain. We *chose* to perceive with anger and selfishness, without compassion for another's ignorance or confusion. Though our point of view seemed reasonable and justifiable, it was our own negative attitudes and choices that created the pollution which blocked our sense of self-esteem.

As long as you believe others have the power to create or destroy your life, you will continue to create your own pollution, because you will do nothing to assess and adjust your own thoughts, words and behaviors. Blame stops all willingness for self change. You will not want to experience the temporary Dust, preferring instead to live within a fixer-upper with no plans for remodeling.

The pollution can be easily removed. First, we must accept this new idea about self-esteem, for it is through our positive choices that our self-esteem will be revealed to us; our choice of thoughts, our choice of words and our choice of actions.

Be *aware* that self-esteem is whole and complete within you at all times, impenetrable by anything outside yourself. Knowing this, you step across the threshold of a new beginning. You are fully prepared to take the action, to Walk-Your-Talk, which is the final vital step in the remodeling process.

Chapter 6

Action

$\mathbf{W}$alking-Our-Talk means *actively* applying the blue-prints. Our sense of self-esteem is only available through our positive thoughts put to action. We change our negative attitudes to positive attitudes and then act on them.

If you are using the affirmation, "I am lovable," but you hear your doubts bubble up, you would be better off affirming, "Today I will *act* lovable." If an affirmation helps to remind you throughout your day to *act* lovable, then take action on those thoughts and you will become lovable automatically. You will soon surprise yourself with an unplanned affirmation that declares, "I really am lovable!" and you will believe it.

You will know you are lovable because of the actions you have willingly taken in that direction. This knowing is the sense of self-esteem. When you feel honestly lovable because you really have become that way, you will feel worthy of anything you want to achieve. This is the result of Walking-Your-Talk. Wherever you have achieved a goal, there is where you have Walked-Your-Talk. You can rely on it.

Using quality Talk is absolutely essential to succeeding. Otherwise our Walk may lead us into a ditch. I want to emphasize the importance of using good materials when remodeling. Action produces mediocrity and disappointment if it isn't quality action.

Chapter 7

Fear

Taking action by changing our thinking and behaviors creates Dust. Fear is another particle of Dust. We get caught up looking at what we think the outcome will be and we experience fear.

Acting on our fears, we practice dishonesty, deception, greed, co-dependency, nagging and other polished techniques of manipulation and control. These, in turn, create more of the same and keep us stuck.

We tend to think we know it all. We are sure we know how others will react, we are sure we know how situations are bound to end, we are sure we know what will happen. And we use all sorts of examples to prove why we know it all. We cite all of our past misfortunes based on similar circumstances. So sure are we of the accuracy of our negative perceptions about past experiences, that we don't ever question ourselves. If we did, we might see how our negative attitudes and behaviors created those misfortunes.

We have created the idea of a negative reality. Based on this idea, we make the worst decisions possible and suffer the consequences. These consequences could be anything from guilt, self-disrespect and retaliation from others, to violence, murder and suicide.

If you are ready to walk away from this insanity, there is only one way to get over fear. Face your fear, squarely. Ask yourself, "What's the worst thing that could happen?" then take it through to the end, "O.K., then what will happen if that other thing happens? And then? And then?..." Then become willing for the worst to happen. Otherwise, you become imprisoned by your fears. The choice is yours.

I became fearful of flying sometime during college. No amount of affirming, white lighting, sharing or therapy, was successful in changing my attitude and my fear.

At a time when I was planning my vacation, my minister suggested that I face my worst fear about flying. Flying was not the problem; *crashing* was the problem.

The fall from the sky and the crash itself kept me awake most of the night, night after night, a month before my vacation. I kept trying to avoid those thoughts and replace them with new happy thoughts. I did not succeed in this endeavor.

I decided to try what my minister had suggested. I was to allow myself the fearful thoughts and play them all the way through, creating as many different ways to crash as possible. I did that and my thoughts lost their power to keep me awake. I began sleeping through the night. The fear didn't go away, but it no longer affected my sleep.

The night before the flight, I was a total mess, but I got on the plane, regardless. This in itself was a miracle. By the time the plane had taken off and landed four times, my fear of flying was gone and has never returned. If I had not faced my fear head on, I would have canceled my trip in favor of my fear. What an eye-opener for me. I almost chose fear over a vacation.

Chapter 8

Integrity: The Quality Materials

Bringing your thoughts, words and behaviors into Integrity is the kind of action that leads to success—success in relationships, business, recreation, education. It is the answer to the permanent achievement of your sense of self-esteem.

Integrity is a power, not just a virtue. It is in this power that you will experience a sense of self-esteem unlike any you have ever known.

Two definitions of Power as defined by Webster's New Collegiate Dictionary are:

1) Possession of control, authority, or influence *over* something or someone.

2) Ability to create an effect.

When most of us think of having power, we tend to think in terms of the first definition above, having power *over* something or someone. The greatest human desire is to have control of our lives, and we think that in order to accomplish this we must have power over people, places and things. So we consciously and unconsciously begin putting specific power-over techniques to work (i.e. dishonesty, interrogation, guilt, accusations, threats, blackmail).

There is a much easier way to have absolute control of our lives without having power-over. This way is through the power of Integrity, which adheres automatically to the second definition of power; simply—the ability to create an effect.

Consider the power of electricity. Electricity has the ability to create an effect. It has no need to have power over anything, because its power is absolute. It is a cause. It is impersonal in nature. It doesn't decide to work for some and not for others. We cannot beg it into working. It just works, provided its three basic principles are present.

The first of these principles is energy. The energy is the substance of electricity. It exists all the time, waiting patiently to be put into use. The second principle is generation. Generation activates the energy, creates life within it, so to speak. The third principle, conduction, focuses the generated energy, creating the outer manifestation that we experience, such as a light, a fan, television, etc., as long as the conductor is without flaws. Without all three of these principles working together, the power of electricity is unavailable to us; it cannot be manifested outwardly and it seems as if it isn't there at all.

So it is with the power of Integrity. The three principles that contribute to the outer manifestation of Integrity are: HONESTY, the substance of Integrity, GENEROSITY, the activation and life of that substance, and GOODWILL, that which colors the quality of the first two and leads to the outward manifestation that we see.

All three principles must be present. If not, the outer manifestation will not reflect Integrity. For example, Honesty by itself could easily be blame: "I'm going to be honest with you. It's all your fault and I think you are a jerk." Generosity without Honesty or Goodwill is phoniness: co-dependency is created and people feel the falsehood. Goodwill without the aid of Generosity will likely be selfish will: "I wish for you that you become the kind of person I think you should be."

Used together, Honesty, Generosity and Goodwill create real Integrity. It is the power that purifies the formerly polluted thoughts, words and behaviors, and it allows the self-esteem to shine through.

As with electricity, until we have personally plugged into Integrity and experienced the results first hand, we cannot know what it brings us. I have found that the best way to experience the results of Integrity is to practice it when I least want to.

There was a time when I was afraid to be Honest about a situation at work, thinking I might lose my job. I decided to practice my Integrity, disregarding the fear (Dust). Not only did I not lose my job, I was commended for my courage and ended up helping some people who were dealing with the same issue. The result was a sensation within me that virtually shouted, "WOW! I can handle anything." I knew I could even have handled getting fired. I had a sense of freedom, a sense of choice, and for the first time that I can remember, a permanent sense of self-esteem. The exultation of that Integrity has been a part of me since it all happened in 1985. It became the impetus I needed for many other Honesty opportunities later on.

REAL PEOPLE

There is a definite aura noticeable in those who actively pursue Integrity. They are confident in their decisions and actions. They have no secrets, even though there may be incidents that others would surely hide, and they carry few regrets, if any, about their lives. They understand their past mistakes and the mistakes of others without bitterness. They know what it means to feel forgiveness.

They are calm and comfortable in their appearance. This is because they govern their lives by Integrity principles and nothing sways them from their conviction and behavior within these principles. They live in the moment and make each day the best it can be. Conditions around them have no bearing on their thoughts, words or behaviors. They continue to be the kind of people they want to be despite all else.

Regardless of environment, nationality, religious belief or personal circumstance, they achieve their Integrity through the continuous unconditional practice of Honesty, Generosity and Goodwill. It is as simple as that. Honesty, Generosity and Goodwill, practiced consciously in their thoughts and behaviors builds their character. They know that they never need to be dishonest, selfish, nor ill-willed toward others for any reason.

They still experience pain in life, they still make errors in thoughts, words and behaviors. The difference is that their commitment to Integrity makes the errors smaller, less painful, quicker to resolve and easily self-forgiveable. This is because they rarely mean to act without Integrity. The moment they realize they are out of Integrity, they get back on track. They remind themselves that there is no blame and then they take action to get back into Integrity.

People of Integrity realize their own greatness. That is what a sense of self-esteem feels like. They could be executives or garbage collectors; they understand their greatness.

They have no fear of risking to achieve their goals because they know inherently that there is no such thing

as failure. The result is that their personal dreams become reality and they experience a life filled with health,
prosperity and happiness.

Chapter 9

How Does Integrity Make Such A Difference?

NEGATIVE AND POSITIVE MESSAGES

Negative and positive messages are effects, caused by certain beliefs you maintain about yourself. An effect cannot change another effect. Causes are the only things that can change effects. Therefore, a positive message cannot change a negative message, though many people seem convinced that it can. They attempt this through the incorrect use of affirmations. When it doesn't work for them, they claim that, "affirmations don't work."

Let's get specific. After making an affirmation that you are lovable and deserving, you then go about your day punishing everyone for not doing what you think they ought to do. You snap at your spouse, yell at the kids, drive inconsiderately in traffic, complain about your boss, gossip, lie, pilfer from work, leave the waiter a stingy tip, act like a martyr, curse your fellow human beings and often wish things upon them that even Attila the Hun wouldn't have thought of.

In other words, when things aren't going the way you want them to go, you are mean, nasty, ill-willed toward others, greedy, dishonest, pouting, blaming and self-righteous; and then you wonder why you don't feel loving and deserving! How can you continue to believe you are lovable and deserving when all the evidence seems to be against you? You wouldn't choose that kind of person for a best friend, so how can you expect to like yourself any better?

You probably don't intend to be that way, and in your heart you think of yourself as an O.K. person, perhaps even a "do gooder." In reality, you are. But when fear sets in and conditions outside yourself disturb you, you react with negative thoughts and behaviors much like the ones mentioned above. Then all of your negative messages, your thoughts and feelings of unworthiness—the pollution—begins to form.

You gave yourself a great positive message, "I am lovable...." But this did nothing to really make you lovable. You must make the ultimate decision to *be* lovable, without regard to outer circumstances. This means contemplating new ways of thinking and behaving concerning people and situations.

No matter how justified you believe your negative thoughts and behaviors to be, no matter how much you affirm your goodness, your Still Small Voice will continuously announce your actual character (which, in this case is unlovable).

STILL SMALL VOICE

The Still Small Voice (as it is referred to in the Bible) is our inner informant. It tattles to us, about us. We cannot hide from it. It alone knows all that we think, say and do. It alone knows our true motivations, the real reasons behind our thoughts, words and actions. It helps us to be aware so that we can adjust our thinking and behaviors to our best advantage for spiritual and personal growth.

The Still Small Voice is our greatest advisor. Its advice is always along the lines of Honesty, Generosity and Goodwill. It lets us know when we are missing the mark by that little gnawing, nagging feeling we have when we know we are wrong or mistaken about something and we don't want to admit it. If the guidance we hear is encouraging us to be dishonest, selfish or ill-willed, we can be certain it is our Ego talking.

The Ego is that part of each of us that wants to believe we are, in some way or all ways, better than others. It wants to believe that we are more special, more beautiful, more intelligent, more spiritual, more normal, more right.

The Ego gets very frustrated when the Still Small Voice tells it the truth. It is at these times that the Ego will want to do anything it can to prove itself right, to try to attain power-over the Still Small Voice. Power-over techniques are dishonesty, selfishness and ill-will. The individual who prefers the Ego over the Still Small Voice will find themselves lying, cheating, manipulating, controlling, taking from, arguing, yelling, using foul language, hating, stealing and often resorting to violent behaviors. And passive aggression is just as much a part of the Ego as violence.

When we decide to prefer our Still Small Voice over our Ego, the Still Small Voice reminds us of our greatness. We realize immediately that we have no need for power-over. We automatically choose Honesty over dishonesty, Generosity over selfishness and Goodwill over ill-will.

In 1986, my spouse and I began a computer consultation business at home. We had little or no money to begin with and we relied on a business loan to help us fund our computer and printer. The amount of software we believed we needed cost more money than we had available.

We would hear people say things such as, "There's a lot of competition out there." We would then buy into that attitude—that we have to be better than someone else in order to make it. Fears over money convinced us to prefer the Ego over the Still Small Voice (which was telling us Honesty was the best policy). I wanted to believe that with all my heart but I was terrified and decided to act on my fears instead of my Integrity.

In frustration, my mind began to look for an answer through dishonesty. Copying this particular software is illegal. Nevertheless, I thought of calling up an acquaintance (who I knew had the software we wanted) and asking her to dinner. "Oh, and by the way, would you mind bringing so-and-so software for us to look at?" (I really meant "have.") My entire motivation for inviting her to dinner was to get her software without having to pay for it. And ...I liked her. I wanted to see her. But the bottom line was the software. The real motivation for the invitation was dishonest and selfish. I was willing to ask my friend to lose her Integrity so that I could lose mine.

Now, I know this is a common practice. The "Everybody does it" excuse may be O.K. for some. But for me, to illegally copy software is deadly to my personal growth. For me, to allow manipulative, dishonest motivation to back my Generosity (the dinner invitation) is the beginning of a life of constant struggle and ultimate mediocrity of character.

This one little infraction will live on inside me. No matter how much I pretend it won't, it will. And it will be there when I want something special for my life. This one little infraction is pollution and it won't go away until I clean up my character. It will blind me from my greatness which is shining brightly on the other side of the pollution. I could become a billionaire through dishonesty, but I will never feel good about me. My money would be used on psychiatrists and analysts. I would always know that I stepped on others in order to get what I wanted. My spirit would be crippled.

As it happened, my Still Small Voice communicated with me loudly and clearly. Heartburn, headache and irritability are effective in getting my attention. When I feel lousy, I look for a lack of Integrity somewhere and I usually find it. In this case, I was reacting to my dishonesty and selfishness. When I realized that I was getting out of Integrity with myself and my friend, I consciously made the decision to cancel the original invitation. She eventually came over for lunch. I made it a point not to ask for software. Even when it was offered, I turned it down graciously.

I overcame my fear of not having enough in order to keep my Integrity. I had been afraid that we would lose our business without the software. We didn't lose a thing. Eventually, we had the money and purchased what we wanted. Shortly thereafter, I had the opportunity to share my experience with a client, who was in a similar situation. His story appears in a later chapter.

The personal power I feel as the result of my Integrity has enabled me, over and over, to ask ample payment for my services. In addition, I do great things for myself today.

If you are sneaky and manipulative, your Still Small Voice will tell you; if you are selfish and dishonest, it will tell you; if, in your heart, you wish punishment on others, it will tell you. Conversely, if you are Honest, Generous and Goodwilled, regardless of outer circumstances, it will tell you that, too. The choice is yours. Your decision is all that is necessary.

TODAY, TODAY, *TODAY*

You can begin to feel great about yourself today. You can experience your true self-esteem in the next minute. All you have to do is commit yourself to Honesty, Generosity and Goodwill, unconditionally, right now. This means that you have decided to walk in those directions and that you are willing to clean up dishonesty, selfishness and ill-will toward everyone to the best of your understanding each day, from this moment on.

At home, in business, during leisure time, at all times, bring your thoughts, words and behaviors into the arena of Honesty, Generosity and Goodwill. Do this with unconditional conviction, and listen for the new messages.

The messages you receive from your Still Small Voice today, whether they are positive or negative, are determined by the person you are today. CHANGE YOUR THOUGHTS, WORDS AND BEHAVIORS TODAY, AND YOU WILL BE FREE OF THE PAIN OF YESTERDAY.

Whatever negative attitudes you hold, acknowledge

them. Then create a positive attitude to replace it. The truth is freeing, not binding. A negative attitude is binding, therefore it cannot be truth. Find a thought that is freeing and you have found the truth.

Yesterday will cease to haunt you as you make new choices today. Nothing anyone did or said to you, will do or will say to you, has anything to do with the self-esteem you feel today. It is all in your own hands, today. What a breath of fresh air.

Chapter 10

The Powers Of Integrity

Honesty
Who we really are

Generosity
What we do with who we are

Goodwill
The motive behind what we do with who we are

Dishonesty, Selfishness and Ill-will are the culprits behind all of our difficulties in life. These are the power-over techniques that cause so much trouble. Lies, deception, cheating, stealing, manipulation, hypocrisy and more come under the heading of dishonesty. Self-seeking, withholding, greed, punishing, abuse, taking from, retaliating and more come under the heading of selfishness. Wishing harm, hating, negative attitudes and blame are all a part of ill-will.

Whatever problems we are having with others, we are experiencing the pain as the result of our own attempts at power-over; *even when it is only in our thinking.* These are all thoughts and behaviors that keep us in a state of mediocrity. In order to break through this wall of negativity, we guide our thoughts and behaviors along the principles of Honesty, Generosity and Goodwill, unconditionally. Unconditionally means "no matter what."

Think of Honesty, Generosity and Goodwill as one umbrella. Standing under it, that is, conforming our thoughts and behaviors to fit within the boundaries of it, will keep us from getting soaked with the consequences of dishonesty, selfishness and ill-will.

Still believing that dishonesty, selfishness and ill-will had the power to make our lives better, we have often been indecisive about which to use; Honesty or dishonesty; Generosity or selfishness, Goodwill or ill-will. This indecision has been confusing and painful. We have always known the best answer, but we allowed our fears and insecurities to rule our better judgment.

We now understand that Integrity is the only power that can make our lives better. It is impossible for it to do otherwise. With this in mind, we strive for the courage to apply Integrity principles to every situation in our lives, bar none.

HOW DOES GOD FIT IN?

Truth, Life and Love are often described as the main aspects of God. Everyone prefers Truth over deception, Life over stagnation and Love over vindictiveness. God is Truth, God is Life, God is Love. These are lovely catch phrases and they look nice on posters and greeting cards, but how does one experience Truth? How do we *do* Life? We hear a lot of talk about Unconditional Love, but what exactly does that mean?

We are spiritual beings in human experiences. Truth, Life and Love are spiritual concepts and must be demonstrated through our human experience. As humans, we have been endowed with specific ways to do this.

The answer lies in Honesty, Generosity and Goodwill. We can *be* Honest, and this creates understanding which will manifest as Truth; we can *be* Generous, and this creates circulation which will manifest as Life; we can *be* Goodwilled, and this creates positive attitudes which will manifest as Love. We can focus all of our thoughts, words and behaviors in the direction of Honesty, Generosity and Goodwill. Honesty is the only way we can actively be Truth. Generosity is the only way we can actively experience Life. Goodwill is the only way we can actively manifest Love. In upcoming chapters, each of these is described in depth.

GOOD INTENTIONS

Most people intend to be Honest, and surely the great majority are not thieves. Most people intend to be Generous and would effortlessly give of themselves when they perceived need. Most people intend to be Goodwilled and prefer to think well of others rather than negatively. But when others fall short of our expectations or we perceive there is no need, excuse-making and rationalizations break down our good intentions. We believe that power-over is justified at certain times. Our intentions become quite conditional in nature. The goal for character building is to practice Honesty, Generosity and Goodwill regardless of the outlying conditions.

Although we think of ourselves as Honest people, a little detective work will reveal the practice of a multitude of little (and sometimes big) dishonesties throughout our day. The same goes for Generosity and attitudes of Goodwill. Real Integrity is: Honesty without excuses, Generosity without attachments or payoff, and Goodwill toward all, no matter what. Honesty only when it's safe, Generosity only when it's convenient, Goodwill only when it's deserved do not reflect Integrity at all.

There is no character growth in conditional Integrity. Living a life of Integrity means practicing Honesty even in the presence of fear, practicing Generosity even in the illusion of lack, and practicing Goodwill even in the appearance of wrongdoing. We must understand that fear is only our reaction to what we *perceive* is happening or what we *perceive* may happen. Lack is only an illusion based on our point of view. Our idea of wrongdoing is a judgment based on things we believe about life. When we realize this and see that there are other realities, we cease to feel the need to protect ourselves.

When most of us first begin practicing Honesty we are doing so in blind faith. The fear is still present, but we walk through it because we realize that fear is only an illusion. With time, the illusion disappears entirely. We are, however, always faced with new challenges as we go through life, and new fears must be confronted and challenged on a daily basis.

As we practice Generosity to the best of our understanding each day, we overcome the fear of not having enough. Every day, a new opportunity for overcoming that fear becomes available to us. But if we act on our fear and become selfish and greedy, we never give the universe a chance to prove itself.

By practicing attitudes of Goodwill regardless of conditions, we begin to take on a powerful feeling of understanding concerning ourselves and the world around us. We become able to see situations more clearly and decision-making is not clouded by judgments, negative thinking and fear. We have direction. When we allow ourselves to harbor negative wishes toward others, under any circumstances, we can achieve nothing more than mediocrity in our life. Regardless of what appears to be success at surface perspective, there will always be an element which holds us back from our desired good. Direction will be sporadic and questionable.

Change means re-thinking, remodeling ourselves from the very foundation. The problem with our former attempts at creating better lives was that we were trying to build a new structure on the old, cracked foundation. The result was a conditional building. It stood just fine until the ground around it shook. Then it collapsed and we were back to where we were before. There was no Integrity. We may have used the best blueprints and materials available. We may have immersed ourselves in active remodeling. But because the cracked foundation was never replaced, nothing could be permanent. This is where we have stumbled. Our self-renovation has not been permanent because our thinking is still embedded in the negatives.

When we begin to examine our thinking, we must be willing to scrape out our old ideas entirely. Everything we believe that leaves thoughts of fear, lack and blame must be scrapped. In other words, we must concede that they are erroneous thoughts. The Truth sets us free. Since fear does not set us free, any thoughts that create fear must not be true. The same goes for thoughts of lack, blame and wrongdoing.

This idea shoots holes through the way most of the world thinks and lives. It means that we can no longer rely on appearances, but must go deeper to find reality. Though this may seem to be swimming against the tide, it is just the opposite. We were actually swimming against the tide before. The evidence is in the pain so many of us have suffered. Though a riptide may seem to be carrying us deeper into the sea, by allowing it to carry us, we eventually find calm waters and swim safely to shore. Our instincts rebel against this. Our fearful tendency is to want to fight the tide. We usually become worn and burned out. So, we learn to ignore our fear instincts and practice Honesty, Generosity and Goodwill even when we think they will drag us out to sea. Those of us who have done it can testify that it works.

When we can look at ourselves in the mirror and see an unconditionally Honest person, we like the person we see. When we have given freely of ourselves, we feel good within ourselves. When we can separate an individual from their negative behavior, refusing to cast attitudes of blame and revenge toward them, we know compassion and feel love. We feel the active love emanating from ourselves and it looks good on us. When the person in the mirror becomes the person we would choose as our very best friend, we know that we have blown away the pollution and we are introduced to our abundant self-esteem.

When we have made the decision to focus all of our thoughts, words and behaviors under the umbrella of Honesty, Generosity and Goodwill, and then we *do* it, we experience our greatness. We know what it means to recognize our self-esteem, and our lives take an immediate turn for the best. It is the difference between a life of mediocrity and a life of greatness.

Chapter 11

Making The Change

PREPARATION FOR CHANGE

With a positive attitude, remodeling can be humorous and fun. It is simple, once the blueprints are prepared. To prepare them, these are the first considerations: what parts of your home are now inconvenient and causing discomfort? Is there a crack in the foundation? Does the roof leak? Do you need larger rooms? Is your kitchen conversation dotted with "excuse me's?" Do your temporary fixes look shoddy?

Once you've decided what needs to change, begin to look for the replacements. Take a good look at your options. What is available? Do you like what Aunt Gertrude and Uncle Barney did with their home? Sometimes we check with a specialist in remodeling. We let them know what we want changed and they can give us ideas. Then we take what we like and leave the rest.

When the unwanted areas have been identified and their replacements planned, we *begin* the process of building. We don't wallpaper the walls until we've removed the old wallpaper. We don't paint over nails or electrical outlets. (Or do you?)

When we're remodeling our lives, the process is the same. It's not that easy? You're right. It's not. Do it anyway. Become aware of the thoughts, words and behaviors that are not, at this time, fitting under the umbrella of Honesty, Generosity and Goodwill.

Look for dishonesty, selfishness, greed, fear, ill-will and other negative attitudes. One of the ways to do this is to look at your personal relationships with others. Where are you uncomfortable? Where is there resentment, anger, self-righteousness, fear, guilt, blame? Wherever you find this discomfort, you will find your own dishonesty, selfishness or negative attitudes. If you are willing to look at yourself, you will find the areas where you lack Integrity.

This self-examination and search is not intended to be a self-punishment. On the contrary. Getting honest with yourself about your negative thoughts and behaviors is the first step in becoming aware of how you have been abusing yourself. It means you are about to discover all of the healthy things you can begin doing for yourself from this moment on.

If you find yourself feeling resistant or uncomfortable in this search, remember that this is natural. There is always Dust when we remodel. The Dust will be swept up or dispersed and blown away naturally. It is temporary. Keep this in mind as you move through this experience.

Get out a piece of paper and make a list, just as if you were going around your house preparing for remodeling. When your list has a few items on it, consider the replacements. Write down each replacement next to the item you want to change. When you catch yourself in the act of the old "stuff," you have been presented with an opportunity. This is the turning point. The decision is yours. Honesty, Generosity and Goodwill are your blueprints. How do your new thoughts, words and actions measure up?

HERE WE GO

Apply the replacements. Experience whatever Dust may come as the result of your change and hold on. This is where affirmations really come in handy. For instance, if you are faced with a situation where you want to choose dishonesty, you might say to yourself, "The outcome of Honesty is always for my highest good."

A friend of mine recently shared her experience with me:

> I was approached by a co-worker who accused me of making an error in record keeping that caused some serious difficulties at work. Upon examination of the situation, I found that it was her error, not mine. I was very angry and upset and feared that my boss would blame me for her error. I didn't know what to do. It was obviously my co-worker's error, but I was feeling guilty and afraid for myself.

> Accepting that I must be out of Integrity somewhere if I'm feeling discomfort, I began to assess myself. I realized that I had been somewhat careless in my record keeping and there was the possibility that any mistakes I had made would be found out in addition to the mistake made by my co-worker. Though I had not made the error that caused this particular problem, I could have. And I feared that the mistakes I'd made that no one knew about were going to be discovered.

> The answer, which worked to relieve my fear and guilt, was to bring myself into Integrity. Affirming the power that exists within Integrity, I went to my boss, along with my co-worker, to explain what had happened. I also admitted that I had not been conscientious about my own record keeping. I offered to spend a couple of weekends or whatever it took, to examine the files and clean up any discrepancies.

> My co-worker remained silent. My first reaction was to be angry with her for not offering her assistance in this endeavor. I heard myself wish that she be fired. Upon hearing my judgmental, ill-willed thoughts, I made a decision to look at her from another angle. I

realized she was very frightened. I put myself in her place and tried to imagine what she was feeling without the knowledge and aid of Integrity principles. This created a feeling of compassion within me and my anger melted. I was freed emotionally, mentally and physically.

My friend had been out of Integrity through selfishness (not putting out the effort in her original record keeping), dishonesty (hiding the fact that she had not done her work well) and ill-willed (blaming her co-worker and hoping that she'd be fired). That is why there was fear and guilt present within a situation that seemingly had nothing to do with her. Upon getting into Integrity, risking her reputation and possibly her job, she experienced the power of Integrity—her self-esteem.

As we replace dishonesty, selfishness and ill-will with Honesty, Generosity and Goodwill, we build our Integrity; and building Integrity means building character. When we base our actions on Integrity, we experience the sensation of self-esteem and the result is a clear and focused direction.

Unconditional Integrity is the foundation for building character. When we are committed to Integrity principles, we choose to walk through fear. As this happens, our Still Small Voice says, "Good for you!" and our personal circumstances automatically begin to change, sometimes quickly, sometimes not so quickly, but they do begin to change.

Applying Integrity to my life was powerful enough to transform my life from fear, unhappiness and uncertainty to confidence, joy and direction. It will do the same for you.

The following sections focus on the three principles of Integrity—Honesty, Generosity and Goodwill. They are included to provide direction and stimulate your efforts in taking action. As you apply them, I encourage you to share your discoveries with others. Giving it away will help you to keep it.

Chapter 12

Honesty

P erhaps the best way to begin a discussion on Honesty is to focus on dishonesty. This is where our search must begin if we are to scrape out the old foundation that is causing the constant collapse of our structure. Where are the cracks? Where is the cement not mixed properly? Are there pieces of the old foundation that are getting in the way of the new concrete?

Where are we disguising dishonesties with rationalizations and excuses in order to make them seem Honest? There are many subtle ways in which we practice dishonesty without even realizing it. Then we suffer the consequences (which could manifest as just about anything) and wonder why we are so uncomfortable.

Usually, our first reaction is to point our finger at something outside ourselves for that discomfort. This is commonly known as blame. "If only so and so wasn't saying this," or "didn't do that..." In fact, we have set ourselves up for the pollution. There is something that we believe or something that we have done that is not based in truth. As mentioned earlier, we usually intend to be honest. We simply are unaware of what we are doing, saying or thinking that is not based in truth.

The key to overcoming the pollution is in your commitment. As long as you are committed to finding and expressing the truth, to the best of your understanding, your pollution will clear.

WHAT *IS* THE TRUTH? SELF-HONESTY

In order to ascertain truth in a given situation, we must:

1) concede that our current judgments and attitudes may not be accurate.

2) remember that the truth creates a feeling of freedom; otherwise it cannot be truth.

We ask ourselves which of our thoughts, opinions or judgments create, within us, a feeling of fear, resentment, anxiety, blame, guilt or self-righteousness. These are our erroneous thoughts and beliefs. There is no reality in them, but they create a very real sense of pain. When we understand that there is a different reality, one that feels good, we look for that reality instead.

For example: the glass of milk can be half-empty or it can be half-full. Assuming that we wish it to be full, we create a positive direction for our feelings by looking at what we have, rather than at what we don't have. This is as much the truth as the negative attitude. The difference is that the truth frees us from concern and allows us the ability to think clearly. A cleared head is much more resourceful at finding a way to fill the glass of milk completely.

The truth frees us emotionally, mentally and physically. Any statement that is not freeing for any reason whatsoever is not truth. There is a different reality, if only we are willing to look for it.

For years we have all accepted opinions and judgments about people, places, things and situations that lean toward the negative. These opinions and judgments often seem perfectly logical, reasonable and without alternative. *But for those of us who want to move beyond mediocrity and into greatness in our lives, these opinions and judgments are dead weight.* We want to transcend these ideas. We want to be aware of the big picture, not just the simple perspective that we see at the moment.

This means that when we become aware of some discomfort within our lives, we question our own beliefs, first. We examine what we think about a given person or situation before taking any action. If those thoughts are not positive in nature, any actions we take will be based on negative or cracked foundation. The structure that is built on it, no matter how solid the materials, will fall apart at the first quake.

It is imperative that we recognize and accept the futility of our negative opinions and judgments. When we do, we are willing to create new positive attitudes and apply them. Our actions will then be based on Integrity, and the outcome will be for the best. Here is an example from a man who was determined to reach a new level of personal Integrity:

> There is this guy at work who continually makes put-down remarks to me. We have little or no contact with one another so I don't know why he persists with his comments. I found myself dreading work each day. My first reaction was to strike back and find the ultimate put-down that would shut him up. Luckily, I managed to remain self-composed, though inwardly, I was angry all the time. I went home feeling drained and could not shake the feeling over the weekend.
>
> I realized that I was blaming him for my discomfort and anger. I wanted to continue to blame him, but I knew that nothing would change inside me if I did. Even though I was suffering from a bad case of self-righteousness, I became willing to question my own beliefs and attitudes.
>
> I asked myself what it was that I thought about him. Here were some of my responses: "He's a jerk; he's a stupid, insecure SOB; he ought to be dead; someone

should get him fired."

All of my beliefs and attitudes were negative and angry in nature. I wrote them out in a list format and took a good look at them. They were easier to objectify like this and I was able to see myself a bit better. Is this what is inside of me? It must be. I decided to concede that none of these beliefs or attitudes were true. They sure seemed true, but they couldn't be. They had me in bondage.

I looked at each one individually and created a new thought for it; one that was positive in nature and could also feel as true as my angry thoughts. This took me a while for some of them. Here are some of the changes: For "He's a jerk," I came up with "He's got nice hair;" for "He's a stupid, insecure SOB," I came up with "He's always on time to work and very reliable as an employee;" for "He ought to be dead," I decided on "He ought to get a promotion;" for "Someone should get him fired," I came up with "Someone should ask him out to lunch."

The humor alone relieved a great deal of the anxiety I was feeling and I suddenly felt released from the fear. I went to work the next day with an entirely different outlook. When he began chiding me, I noticed his hair. I watched how hard he worked. I thought about suggesting a promotion for him (though I have no jurisdiction in that area). Then I asked him to join me for lunch. He was surprised to say the least, but smiled and agreed. We now go fishing together at least once a month. He still makes his remarks. I make them back and we both smile a lot.

Not all relationship problems are that easily solved,

but all self-esteem problems are that easily solved. Even if their relationship had not improved, my friend would have still been introduced to the highest part of himself through his Integrity. His self-esteem would be shining through and the behaviors of the antagonist would have ceased to bother him.

This aspect of Honesty, self-Honesty, is the cornerstone for everything that follows. By replacing our negative beliefs and attitudes with positive beliefs and attitudes (Truth), we create the foundation for Integrity. Otherwise, it would be like trying to produce electricity without energy.

BLAME

Blame is the insistence that something outside ourselves has control over or responsibility for our personal circumstances. Since nothing outside ourselves has that control or responsibility, blame is, within itself, an untruth.

Blame is self-righteousness. Self-righteousness is at the root of every one of our negative attitudes, opinions and judgments. And those attitudes, opinions and judgments can be summed up in one word—WRONG. We are angry because something or someone has done something wrong according to our personal ideas and beliefs.

Blame completely obliterates our freedom of choice. From the moment we even think blaming thoughts, we have become attached to whatever we are blaming, carrying it with us in the forms of excuses and rationalizations. This is where so many people become paralyzed in their efforts to grow out of their problems. Since they are dragging around so much unnecessary baggage, they cannot move freely.

Blame makes decision-making virtually impossible. We base our decisions on what someone or something else is doing, has done or will do. When we are willing to stop blaming under all circumstances, we release the power of choice into our control. We choose our own thoughts. We choose our own words. We choose our own actions. No longer are we confused and frustrated about decisions. When our inner guidance is supported by the desire for Integrity, our choices reflect that Integrity.

MOTIVES

Getting Honest about our true motive is absolutely essential. I use the word "motive" instead of "motives" because it is necessary to acknowledge the one main reason behind any decision we make. It is very easy to allow a series of healthy motives to hide the one unhealthy motive that is really behind the decision. Here is a story related to me by a minister:

> One of our congregation members gave us a computer. Another member came in with a few software programs he had in his own collection at home. He was willing to copy these programs onto our blank disks and xerox the instructions for us. This way, our church would not have the burden of buying these expensive programs.

I vaguely sensed that there was a dishonesty problem here, but I began to rationalize. After all, the fellow had already purchased the programs himself. He should have the option of giving copies to anyone. After all, we're a church. It's not like he's selling them to make money. After all, it will help so many people. After all the after alls, I allowed him to do the copying.

There was a constant, nagging feeling in the pit of my stomach that said, "Something's not right here." Finally, I had to get down to the truth about the reason, the real reason, I gave my O.K. to a dishonest situation. The truth was, I was afraid to spend the money we had on software because we had some other needs that were pressing. Rather than have faith that God would provide everything we needed at the perfect time (like I tell my parishioners to do), I lost my Integrity. When I realized my mistake, I erased the illegal copies and returned the copied manual.

I felt cleansed and experienced a strong sense of self-esteem. I used this incident in a future sermon. Within an hour after the sermon, quite unexpectedly, the money for all of the software we needed was donated anonymously. In addition, a fund for the computer was set up.

I had never before taken a good look at the real motive behind my decisions. It proved to be spiritually uplifting and strengthening. I no longer suffer with the decisions I make because I know, if they have Integrity, they must be the best they can be.

There had been many good reasons to allow a dishonesty. The Still Small Voice knew the real reason behind the decision. It continued to send messages that there was a crack in the foundation. Had the minister not replaced the foundation, the structure (church's Integrity) would have been weak and vulnerable. It would *seem* unrelated to the computer. That's the way it usually happens. If there is a lack of Integrity in one area, there is probably a lack of Integrity in other areas.

This brings us back to the concept of beliefs and attitudes. If they are positive in nature, then that is how others will see us. If there is negative inside, it will eventually show on the outside in some capacity. We cannot hide our real character.

"CASH REGISTER" HONESTY

If you are the kind of person who is meticulous about not stealing anything in any way, shape or form, then you practice "Cash Register" Honesty.

"Cash Register" dishonesty is the phrase I use to describe any kind of stealing (i.e. money, items, pilfering, breaking copyright laws, ideas, cheating on taxes, not reporting taxable income and especially taking advantage of someone's mistake). This applies whether or not someone owes you or you believe they ought to owe you. If there has been no legal resolution or moral agreement giving you ownership, it is stealing, PERIOD, no matter how small.

Our thoughts and words apply here just as much as our actions. If you spend time thinking about getting away with stealing or discussing it even as idle conversation, you may have stealing intentions. Though an opportunity has not come about for you to apply your intentions safely, you harbor the idea and, given the right situation, you might go through with it. Even if your Still Small Voice bugged you enough so that you changed your mind, you would resent your Still Small Voice for being there. This is being a thief at heart.

You can attempt to steal more than just physical goods. You can steal another person's place in line, another person's turn to talk, another person's time. You can steal a parking place (have you ever felt cheated when someone took up more than one space in a crowded parking lot?). You can steal someone's peace and quiet or their view at a theater.

Cash register dishonesty is an easy place to start when searching for dishonesties. It means looking at the ways in which you are inconsiderate. It means looking at all of the times you try to get away with things. What you may not realize is that you never get away with anything. Your Still Small Voice remembers all and makes regularly scheduled broadcasts at the times when you least want to hear distressing news.

"CHERRY TREE" HONESTY

Almost every child has been told the story of George Washington and the cherry tree. To refresh your memory, young George wanted to use his brand new axe and found the perfect victim: the cherry tree in front of his home. When his father noticed the tree looking a bit different than usual, he confronted George with the question, "Did you chop down the cherry tree, son?" George courageously stood up and said, "I cannot tell a lie. I did it with my little axe." He then went on to become the first president of the United States of America. Just a coincidence?...

If you "cannot tell a lie," you practice "Cherry Tree" Honesty. This assumes that, to the best of your understanding, you do not alter or withhold any part of the truth as you understand it from anyone for any reason.

This does not mean we tell our life's story to strangers. There is an element of common sense to be applied here. Occasionally, we find ourselves in a position of uncertainty. We're not sure whether or not it is necessary to reveal certain information to certain people at certain times. Usually, a check of our motivations will suffice. For instance: it is not our business to reveal someone else's personal information. That becomes gossip. We usually know when the truth is being hidden, omitted, stretched or altered. We can usually ascertain when we are trying to manipulate a person or situation through our dishonesties.

White Lies

Little white lies or convenient lies are good examples of manipulation. If there is no manipulation going on, then there is no reason to lie. Those who are interested in living a life of excellence will take the time to think over gracious ways of telling the truth, rather than set-tling for an easy out with a white lie. White lies cause just as much pollution, weakening our sense of self-es-teem, as out-and-out lies. This is because a lie is a lie. We tend to think that the consequence of the lie deter-mines the degree of legitimacy. A lie is a lie. One per-son's negative consequence could be another person's reward. A lie is a lie. And our sense of self-esteem pays the price.

COMMITMENT

We can make a commitment to Honesty as a way of life if we believe that there is a positive Honest answer for every situation. If we are really serious about creat-ing a life of greatness, we will seek to find that answer.

Honesty is a lifetime exercise. The sooner we get on a regular schedule, the sooner we reap the benefits. We begin by choosing those areas where we are ready to clean up dishonesties and then we do it.

Chapter 13

Generosity

T he word "Generous" derives its current meaning from the Latin word "genus," which means "birth." Where there is birth, there is life. No birth, no life. If we want to experience living, we must birth or create life. Generosity means to generate, to circulate. Blood circulates; without that circulation, there is no experience of life.

This is what generosity is really all about. It's giving and it's more than giving; it's kindness and it's more than kindness; it is the impetus for life.

GENEROSITY IS FUN

It is human nature to want to generate, to be an active part of life. Children are especially in touch with this.

Have you ever been to a playground where there are children playing on a merry-go-round? The merry-go-round is one of those rides that has to be started by someone in order for it to operate. Usually, young children who don't know how to generate the ride will sit on it and wait for a generator. An older child will come along and begin to push it around. Once it is going well on its own, the older child will jump on and enjoy the ride. Many times, the younger children, having learned what to do, will attempt to do the pushing. They have an insatiable desire to join in and become a part of the cause. They want to create life in the ride.

Have you ever seen young children pushing their stroller instead of sitting in it? They are not interested in what they will receive as payment. They simply want to be a part of the generation. It's *fun*.

Somewhere along the way to adulthood, many of us have forgotten that true Generosity is great fun. It satisfies our natural desire to create life, it allows us to accumulate a wide variety of experiences and memories and it always circulates back to us. This is the natural outcome of Generosity.

If your life seems stagnant or boring, examine the

status of your Generosity. How do you participate in life? There are religious organizations, political organizations, health clubs, schools, jobs, volunteer work, etc., all of which could not exist without the Generosity of the people who attend. They are Generous simply by their attendance. A meeting is only a meeting if the individuals show up. The same holds true for all functions where people make the function happen. And these are the places where friendships are established. From there, even more life can be created.

Do you attend movies, concerts, plays, parades, classes; or do you make excuses such as, "I can't afford it," "I don't have time," "I'm too tired," "I don't want to go alone," etc.? Have you made the effort to call someone? Or are you waiting for people to call you?

What do you birth or bring forth into the world? Where do you create and support life? How do you give of yourself, your time and your substance without expectation of repayment? Don't allow your fears and excuses to plug up your circulation and inhibit the experience of living fully. Go for it!

GENERATING PROSPEROUS RELATIONSHIPS

Wherever we go and whatever we do, we are in a relationship with something or someone. This could be other human beings, animals, plants or inanimate objects. Are your relationships prosperous? Prosperous means vigorous and healthy growth. Is there healthy growth in your relationships? Do you take good care of your part in your relationships?

Generosity With Inanimate Objects

Let's say you buy a waterbed. The instructions say to clean the mattress a certain way with a specific substance twice a month. You decide that it's too much trouble to do and you ignore the instructions. One year later, your bed begins to leak and it isn't coming from the seams. Your first reaction is to blame the waterbed or the factory that made it, the salesperson or the store where it was purchased.

You probably drag the deflated mattress down to the shop, along with the warranty and the receipt. You're upset for several reasons. You're afraid they are going to tell you what you already know—that the problem came from improper treatment. You also see yourself having to purchase a new mattress.

Let's say the worst happens. They point out to you that the mattress hasn't been treated properly. Do you admit your part in the problem? Or are you blaming the mattress? It's time to get in touch with the truth. Your lack of care within your relationship with the mattress short-changed that relationship. What could you have done differently with the mattress that might have prevented the leak?

When we enter into an agreement with an inanimate object by purchasing it, there needs to be a commitment on our part with the item purchased. Since it cannot take care of its own maintenance, we must be willing to do for it what it cannot do for itself. This is a form of Generosity. By cleaning and revitalizing the object in some way, we create a longer, healthier relationship with it. Without our commitment of Generosity toward the item, our good relationship with it is short-lived.

Is there anything at this time in your life that is not functioning properly? Examine your relationship with it. Do light bulbs need replacing? Screws need tightening? Oil need changing? Carpet need cleaning?

Concerning ourselves about our personal relationships with inanimate objects may seem bizarre. But it makes sense. How much time and energy do you spend in aggravation with things that are malfunctioning? Also, by looking carefully at the way you treat inanimate objects, you may find where you are neglecting Generosity with the people in your life.

Generosity With People

Entering into relationships with people requires a definite commitment of Generosity. If each person is waiting for the other to make the first move, the result is that no one does. We have to stop waiting for the other guy. Greatness of character means taking the steps toward greatness regardless of surrounding circumstances.

People don't always think, say or do what we believe they should. How do we handle ourselves successfully within the relationship when these issues arise? Do we practice power-over techniques, such as pouting, nagging, accusing, manipulating and sarcasm? Or do we give acceptance, understanding, compassion and love?

Prospering Good Relationships

What are the first words you say to the person you live or work with? I know many relationships that took a turn for the better when the first words given or generated were words of appreciation or Generosity. "I'm happy you are in my life today," or "What would you like for breakfast? I'm cooking for you this morning."

When you go to your job, do you take a moment to give words of appreciation to all with whom you come into contact? "I appreciate you, Michael." Even when there doesn't seem to be a reason for appreciation, look for one and communicate.

Bring the boss a cup of coffee even though it's not part of your job description, and bring your assistant the coffee if you are the boss. Have a greeting card waiting on the desk of someone you don't know and ask them to join you for lunch. Do the same for the one person you seem to dislike the most. Do it generously, without expecting anything in payment, not even a "thank you" or change in attitude from them. Find the positive, Generous message that applies to your situation and then USE IT.

Do it because it's the kind of person you want to be. Do it because you want to transcend mediocrity and achieve greatness in your life today.

CO-DEPENDENCY

A discussion on Generosity would not be complete without some comparison to co-dependency. It is Generous to "do unto others" without attaching ourselves to payment. Co-dependency is the act of doing for others so that they will pay us off by: liking us, loving us, thinking of us, leaving us alone, approving of us, treating us well, reciprocating favors, being our ally and so on.

There is a definite expectation of payment. It has been implied that co-dependents are good souls who give too freely of themselves and the takers take advantage of them. Not so! The person who suffers from co-dependency has self-centered expectations of others. Obsessing over another person is self-centered. For one thing, their obsession is to gain control over the other person in some way. For another, the co-dependent person virtually ignores the other people in their lives due to their constant attention on the one. Here is an example from one of my friends:

> One beautiful Saturday morning, my three kids asked
> if we could go to the zoo. It sounded like a great idea so
> we all finished breakfast and hurried to get dressed. As
> we were just about to leave, my husband said he had a
> headache and would prefer staying home. I knew that
> this meant he was staying home so he could eat com-
> pulsively. I wasn't about to let him get away with that
> so I canceled the trip to the zoo. My kids were hurt and
> angry, but I was so obsessed with my husband and his
> overeating that I didn't care. I should have just gone to
> the zoo without him and had a good time with my kids.

This is a form of inverted self-centeredness. Many people who practice this kind of co-dependency see themselves as self-*less*. But this is not really the case. They center themselves on others to control, manipulate and change other people to suit their own personal needs.

Once a practicing co-dependent begins to recover, a new form of self-centeredness often appears. It's called "I'm just going to take care of myself and be good only to me." This is throwing the baby out with the bath water. They are throwing away true kindness along with throwing away manipulation, control, enabling, fixing and rescuing.

Many recovering people are endangering their relationships as the result of this reversed self-centeredness. By doing this, they stop generating life in their relationships and ultimately within their own lives, which is just the opposite of what they intended.

Enabling is the act of taking on someone else's responsibility when you don't want to do it and the person needs to do it for their own personal growth or recovery. This is an excellent example of enabling:

> *My wife would come home from school in an angry mood. She was overwhelmed by the extent of homework that had been assigned. I would jump to the rescue by doing her writing assignments. I hated doing it, but I thought I was being helpful and I expected her to appreciate me. She didn't even change her mood, let alone appreciate my hard work. She ended up failing her final examination because she had never learned the lessons embodied in the assignments. This meant an-*

*other semester of school and the expenses incurred as
the result. Also, it meant another four months without
added income from her employment due to her school
commitment. She blamed me for causing her to fail.*

In this case, it would have been Generous to give the
opportunity of hitting bottom, instead of attempting to
make everything all right. But some people go overboard
even where this is concerned:

*I decided I wanted to assist my son in hitting his bot-
tom. He was a functioning alcoholic. He never vom-
ited, fell or broke anything while he was drunk. I knew
when he would be home and I set a trap for him. Usually, he would come in loudly and awaken my other
children.*

*This time I had it all planned out. I threw some oil on
the pavement leading to the front door in hopes that he
would slip. Then I would point out to him that he was
getting worse, the sign of advancing alcoholism. He
would agree with me out of humiliation and go into a
treatment center.*

*That never happened. Instead, he slipped, hit his head
on the corner of the front porch step and I had to rush
him to the hospital with a broken neck.*

The point here is that it is not up to us to create a crisis or bottom for someone, but to allow them to suffer
the natural consequences of their own decisions and actions.

There is a simple way to determine which is true
kindness and which is co-dependency:

1) Ask yourself if you expect anything from the recipi-

ent of your Generosity in the way of favor, attitude or behavioral change.

2) Ask yourself if you are doing something for them that they must do for themselves for their personal growth, knowledge or recovery.

3) Ask yourself if what you are about to do is dishonest or manipulative.

If you can answer "yes" to any one of these, you are probably practicing co-dependency. If you can answer "no" to all three, you are probably acting out of kindness and Generosity. The true test is in the results. If there is discomfort after giving, there was probably an expectation attached. If there is a feeling of Good having been done, then it was probably Generosity.

The co-dependency is in the motivation, not in the act itself. If you are motivated by the desire to be generous and not by the desire to control or manipulate, the result will be a sense of self-esteem and an enhanced relationship.

Mirror, Mirror...

Our relationships are our best vehicles to character self-assessment. They mirror us. What we loathe in others we can find in ourselves. Similarly, what we love in others, we can find in ourselves. At first it may be difficult to see this, but a little searching will prove the point:

There is this woman that I can't stand. She is whiny

*and complains about everyone. All she ever talks about
are her problems or her negative opinions about others.
She's very selfish and judgmental.*

This is a rather ungenerous view of this person. In other words, the author of this statement is just as whiny and complaining, negative and opinionated, selfish and judgmental as the person he is speaking about. Until he sees this in himself, he will continue to blame the woman for making him uneasy.

The truth is that his discomfort is in his own choice of attitude and perception of this woman. If he is willing to look at himself through her, he will be able to assess and make changes in himself. As he stops his own internal, as well as external, gossiping and judging, he will see her *and* himself in a more compassionate and loving light. He will be free.

Eliminating blame—completely—from all of our relationships is Generosity at it's foundation. Blame creates an environment of stagnation. No one who is blaming will make any changes in themselves. There can be no growth or development in a relationship where there is blame.

It is Generous to look for positive alternative thoughts, words and behaviors about others and then apply them. The original thoughts:

*There is this woman that I can't stand. She is whiny
and complains about everyone. All she ever talks about
are her problems or her negative opinions about others.
She's very selfish and judgmental.*

The change:

> *There is this woman I know. I wish the highest Good*
> *for her .*

HIGHEST GOOD

Highest Good means awakening and enlightenment. When I wish the highest good for others, I am hoping that they are awakened and enlightened about themselves and their relationship to the world. I am deleting the aspect of reward and punishment altogether. I do not mean that we allow people to continue harming others. I mean only to wish that they become healthy in mind and spirit, thereby never harming others again. Can you imagine an enlightened Stalin? Al Capone? King Henry VIII? Marie Antoinette? These people had a knack for leadership. Just think what they could have accomplished with awakening and enlightenment as their foundations. This kind of thinking keeps me clear of anger and resentment and therefore, insanity.

It's very much like creating a new path or hiking trail. Most people are comfortable following the beaten path. When the old path begins to lead into a hornet's nest, the hiker will create a new path.

It isn't always easy or comfortable to change or create a new path at first. Thorny bushes and large rocks often give the illusion that there is no other way. This is the Dust. But faced with a hornet's nest, we are usually willing to create another way. *And there is always another way.*

The better we get at creating new paths or ways of changing our thoughts and attitudes, the easier our lives become. We have freedom. We know there is always an alternative way of viewing every situation in our lives. We can gauge ourselves by the way we react toward others without immersing ourselves in the attempt to change them.

The change in ourselves will transcend any challenges we face. The more we experience this, the simpler and quicker changing becomes. We no longer allow angry thoughts to remain and fester within us because we have the power to release them through our willingness to change ourselves.

GENEROSITY OF SPIRIT

What do we think about others? When someone sings off key do we focus on the bad notes? Many of us do. The person who wants to achieve greatness in character will hear themselves thinking the ungenerous thoughts and will exercise their power of choice to change focus. This person will choose to focus on the positives. This is being Generous in spirit.

What are we willing to give others in spirit? We can give others our good wishes and intentions. We can give compassion and understanding. We can give the benefit of doubt. We can give encouragement.

INVESTING IN THE DREAMS OF OTHERS

Whatever Generosity we invest in others is a Generosity invested in ourselves. The success of one is the success of all. We are individuals, undivided, indivisible. When we allow our jealousies to stand in the way of our Generous wishes toward others' dreams, they stand in the way of our own dreams as well.

Do you ever hear the lack of life and spirit in pessimistic statements? Though the pretext is often in being helpful, there is an underlying negativity that shouts of death. It could be jealousy, pessimism, resentment, selfishness. All of those attitudes are indicative of a plugged-up consciousness. There is no circulation in those statements, no generation of life.

Invest in the dreams and plans of others, regardless of who they are. Invest in the dreams and plans of others, regardless of your opinion of the value of their desire. The way to do this is simple. Wish them the best, support their efforts with your heart. Don't try to fix or help them unless you are asked specifically to do so, or unless you have first asked them if they would like some feedback and they answered "yes." Say nothing negative or forewarning. Wish for them their highest Good. Do this and you will be supporting yourself as well.

PRACTICING GENEROSITY CONSCIOUSNESS

We've explored relationships and ways of assessing our Generous work within them. Generosity is absolutely essential to the happiness and joy of the individual. For this reason, a system of Generosity practice has become an important element within the world's various societies. This system is referred to as "tithing."

Tithing

Every major religious doctrine in the world educates us in the ways of Generosity through the regular practice of tithing. This is no accident. Tithing was developed as a means to create a regular giving/receiving consciousness. The spiritual leaders knew that a positive consciousness of giving *and* receiving created easier, happier and more joyous lives for people. These wise masters understood what unconditional Generosity would produce in those who chose to practice it. So they wrote it into the doctrine.

Unfortunately, some religions have taken advantage of this originally spiritual practice and turned it into an endeavor of greed, rewarding those who tithe and punishing or ignoring those who don't. Nevertheless, the original intent was to enhance the giving and receiving spirit within each of us. It is possible to practice tithing for that spiritual enlightenment in our lives today.

Tithe means one-tenth. Tithing is the act of giving one-tenth of all gross income (this means money) to your source of personal inspiration (not necessarily religious in nature). This could be your church, but it could also be the author of a book that gave you inspiration, a neighbor who gives you inspiration, a song writer, a friend, a family member, institution, etc. The only requirement is that it is given on the basis of inspiration, not need or pity. This means that a millionaire could receive your tithe.

A tithe differs from a gift or a donation. The tithe is an exercise in unconditional Generosity, meaning that we don't base our giving on a particular set of circumstances surrounding the person, place or institution. It takes all of the judgment and opinions out of giving. A gift or a donation is giving beyond that which has already been tithed.

The Benefits of Tithing

If we are having financial difficulties, the problem goes deeper than our current job or salary. It begins in our thinking. We have thoughts of fear and lack. When we withhold ourselves in any capacity due to our belief that we won't have enough, we miss out on the experience of a better life. Tithing regularly, we learn that we will always have enough. This releases us to experience life more fully and without worry.

Tithing to our source of personal inspiration, giving freely and without attachment to the use of that money, we open up a door for ourselves to feel worthy. This must be experienced first hand. The results of feeling worthy are so outstanding and vary so much from individual to individual that it cannot be described in a book. All I can say to you is this—don't miss out on it. Try tithing for a while. See what happens. It's very simple.

Take 10% of your income on payday and give or send

it to a person, place or institution where you have received personal inspiration. If I have received inspiration from more than one source, I sometimes split it between them. Use your own intuition and go with it.

THE RETURN

Even though Generosity means giving freely, without expected payoffs, there *are* returns. This usually comes to us in an unexpected manner, from unexpected sources and at unexpected times. However, there is one return that we can count on: this is the sense of self-esteem that only comes as the result of true Generosity.

Generosity is a large chapter in this book, and with good reason. It is the essence of ACTION. *QUALITY* ACTION. In order to experience, we must do. Generosity is easy because it is natural to us. This concept is embodied extraordinarily well in a simple phrase, "Give until it feels good!"

Chapter 14

Goodwill

Goodwill is the power of Integrity that separates the honey bees from the killer bees. It is the power of love that overcomes all fear. It leads us to experience our greatness and to live a life of fullness and excellence.

MIND-ACTION

Goodwill, like Honesty and Generosity, is a decision; it is an action of the mind. We decide to look at the best

in everyone, no matter who they are or what they may
have done. We take mind-action to wish the highest
Good for everyone regardless of circumstances. This
brings us into alignment with the power of Goodwill and
our lives begin to shine.

Honesty, Generosity and Goodwill together produce
Integrity. It is impossible to practice Honesty and Generosity without Goodwill. Lacking the motivation of
Goodwill, Honesty and Generosity is dishonest and
greedy. Goodwill is the light bulb that allows the energy
to be generated into the light that we see. If the light
bulb is burned out, no amount of energy and generation
will produce light. Once more—Honesty, Generosity and
Goodwill together produce Integrity.

SERENITY—THE NATURAL EXPRESSION OF GOODWILL

Serenity creates the atmosphere for Goodwill to be
expressed naturally. We express Goodwill naturally
when we feel no sense of threat to our well-being; when
we are in a positive state of mind. This feeling of safety
is serenity. When we are serene, we have no trouble
seeing the best and wishing the best for everyone.

There are many instances when we experience serenity without even knowing it. Let's take a look at some of
those aspects of life where we feel serene and Goodwill
is naturally expressed.

The unmistakable exhilaration of a new beginning is

at hand wherever there is a birthday, high school commencement, marriage or promotion. There is a sense of serenity. People are filled with love, hope and good wishes—the natural expression of Goodwill.

Walking through the mall, we stop in the pet store to play with the puppies and kittens. They're all cuddled up together sleeping. "Awwwhhh...," the natural expression of Goodwill.

We walk through the maternity ward at a hospital and feel privileged to view the newborns. We gaze in wonder at the little bodies lying there seemingly helpless. Our hearts are filled with an unconditional love and we may even long to hold one of them. For a moment, our own problems seem very distant and we are serene. We wish each baby health and happiness—the natural expression of Goodwill.

Fear

When we are threatened by the thoughts, words or actions of others, we become fearful and we lose our sense of serenity. Expressions of Goodwill are then hidden behind the pollution of our fear. In order to overcome the fear, a decision must be made to practice the expression of Goodwill unconditionally.

Opening up the heart to practice Goodwill is a matter of willingness and decision-making on the part of each individual. We must be willing to let go of negative attitudes and beliefs, taking the mind-action to replace them with positive attitudes and beliefs.

As with Generosity, the benefits of Goodwill have been recognized as so essential to our personal growth and development, that every social group in the world has a system for the practice of Goodwill. This system is commonly referred to as forgiveness.

FORGIVENESS—THE PRACTICE OF GOODWILL

Forgiveness is an action; it is the act of mentally supporting another person's happiness. To forgive means to wish the best for; it means to give good. This could be good thoughts, good words or good actions. Forgiving means releasing someone or something from our mental, physical, emotional or spiritual punishment. When we wish for others their highest Good, regardless of their negative thoughts, words and actions toward us, we are in the act of forgiveness.

Forgiveness does not deny that there has been pain. It simply says that the pain suffered will not have dominion over our Integrity. We will not allow our pain to dictate the way we think about and treat others.

A few years ago, when I was teaching middle school orchestra, there was a teacher who used the same office area as I did. He rarely had anything positive to say and he made it a point to criticize the other people in that office incessantly. He would get to know what they were sensitive about and make snide remarks or comments to them every time he had an opportunity.

I was one of his targets. One day, after a particularly irritating session with him, I was ready to strike out. Just as I was about to lay into him verbally, he decided to add fuel to the fire. He looked me straight in the eye and said sarcastically, "I have the power to make you hate me, don't I?"

I knew he was right. I hated him. At that moment I realized I could make a choice. I could choose to love him. I began looking at his antics as humorous and actually found myself enjoying him. He must have felt the difference because he kept trying harder and harder to get me to react. He was experiencing the Dust of my remodeling. The more he tried, the more I loved him. It became fun for me and I was released from the pain of my hate. I had forgiven by changing my entire perception of the situation. I no longer felt threatened and I experienced a sense of serenity.

THE PRACTICE OF ILL-WILL

Focusing on the worst in any given situation is practicing ill-will. Ill-will is actually the negative perception we have of a given situation. We have created feelings of fear by our own negative attitudes. In turn, these fears lead us away from Integrity and our actions then follow suit.

We begin to reach for power-over techniques, thinking that they will create the security and serenity that we are seeking. Yet, security and serenity is completely unrelated to power-over techniques. Dishonesty incurs guilt and increased fear, in addition to more dishonesty. It can *never* create real security. It simply trades one form of fear for another.

If our will is ill, our actions will always be questionable. People will feel the insincerity in a variety of ways, though they may not understand what they are feeling. They, in turn, may react to their negative feelings toward us with their own set of power-over techniques. This is where relationship difficulties begin and end.

Focusing our behaviors in the direction of Goodwill is simple. We ask ourselves if our thoughts, words and actions are intended for the highest Good of all concerned. Are we using anyone deceptively? Are we hearing ourselves rationalize and excuse our behavior? If we are uncertain as to whether or not our behavior is ill-willed, we can check to see if we are employing any of these power-over techniques.

Gossip

Gossip is an underhanded way of punishing and getting even. It is a dumping of our deep seated angers and jealousies, and it is the result of frustration. When we think we are somehow unable to control or manipulate a situation the way we would like to, we choose gossip as a replacement. It could be very simple and unassuming gossip, but it is still gossip and the root is still the same—ill-will.

We often look for excuses and justifications in order

to feel O.K. about our gossip. We rationalize in order to appease our Still Small Voice. The Still Small Voice, however, cannot be appeased. It has no decision-making power. It does not choose it's message by virtue of argument. It merely tells the truth, because that is all it knows. If our will is ill, we can count on our Still Small Voice to let us know.

When tempted to gossip, we can redirect the conversation, excuse ourselves from the conversation or state openly that we will not discuss those who are absent. There are many ways to enjoy time with others that do not include gossip. Find them and use them. This is the practice of Goodwill.

But

The word BUT is very convenient when we want to *seem* positive and *be* negative. BUT is a word of argument. It is usually preceded by a YES. "Yes, but..." means that we are going to give the other person one-tenth of a second for acknowledgement of their view. The BUT then negates that view entirely. Refraining from the use of the word BUT is practicing Goodwill.

Self-centeredness

When our fear overwhelms us and we do not understand the power of Integrity (it always brings about the best outcome), we make decisions based on our self-centeredness which are often dishonest and disruptive to the lives of others. We're usually aware of our behavior. We do it anyway because we're scared and are afraid of the alternatives. However, sometimes we are unaware of our self-centeredness.

For instance, we stay at a job that we do not like because we are afraid we will not get something better. We are out of Integrity with our employer because we cannot be doing the best job possible; we are out of Integrity with our fellow employees because we are probably not that enjoyable to be around; we are out of Integrity with our families because we have no energy to give to them (it is all expended in resentment, anxiety, burn-out and a variety of other ills, physical as well as mental); we are out of Integrity with the person who would be just perfect for that job; and, we are out of Integrity with ourselves.

We don't intend to harm these other people. Our fear creates ideas in our heads that we'd better hold on tight and not let go or share. This is the essence of self-centeredness. It means we are so caught up in ourselves that we minimize the pain and needs of others. Taking time to ask how we can be Good-willed with others and then putting that to action is practicing Goodwill.

Other Power-over Techniques

Blame, criticism, judgment and punishment are popular power-over techniques that leave us completely powerless. Rather than change our attitude and look for the Good in a situation, we exercise ill-will. We say to ourselves, "This is bad, and that over there is why it is bad."

Letting go of power-over techniques is as simple as looking for the best in every situation. This is the practice of Goodwill. The need for power-over disappears because our new perception is that everything is in order.

UNCONDITIONAL LOVE

Goodwill toward all people, regardless of who they are or what they have done, is the manifestation of unconditional love. It includes wishing the highest Good, investing in other's dreams and looking for and finding the positive in all people and situations.

Goodwill through unconditional love must begin in our daily lives. If we practice unconditional love within our little households and work-places, our world leaders will learn to practice it at the peace summits. It is this love that opens up the world to peace.

Chapter 15

What's In This For Me?

Honesty attracts Honesty. Generosity attracts Generosity. Goodwill attracts Goodwill. Integrity attracts Integrity. Whatever we put out into the world, we will receive back the same. Any time we think, say or do something negative, we are planting the seed of negativity in ourselves. As it grows and festers within us, that is what we experience in our lives—negativity—mediocrity. Any time we think, say or do something positive, we are planting the seed of positivism. As it grows and feeds us, that is what we experience in our lives—positivism—excellence.

Whatever we think or say about another person, we are actually describing ourselves—like attracts like. Though we may not be able to see it from our own surface perspective, we attract to ourselves those people, things and situations that are most like us in character. Our personalities may be quite different; our character will be the same. Like attracts like.

Greed attracts greed, dishonesty attracts dishonesty, guilt attracts guilt, jealousy attracts jealousy, self-centeredness attracts self-centeredness, self-pity attracts self-pity.

Risk changing all of that! After all, Honesty attracts Honesty. Generosity attracts Generosity. Goodwill attracts Goodwill. Integrity attracts Integrity. Risk the fear and risk the doubt; risk the Dust of remodeling, and do it now. There is so much of life to experience and so much of yourself to contribute to that experience. If I seem overly enthusiastic in my desire to inspire you to QUALITY ACTION, well, that's just me. Pardon My Dust...I'm *Still* Remodeling, too.

Chapter 16

My Own Remodeling

I think I was born with a negative outlook on life. I was teased incessantly in grade school and junior high school and I couldn't detach from the teasers. I hated them. I wished all kinds of harm on them. I'm sure my inner feelings came out in my eyes, because somehow they knew they could always get my goat.

For some unknown reason, high school proved to be much better. I was very active in music and went on to college where I met and married a fellow student. Things seemed to be going along well in my life. We graduated from college and moved to Las Vegas, Nevada, where I became a music teacher. I taught there for six years altogether.

During those years in Las Vegas, a number of traumatic things happened. Within a period of five years, I suffered through some great personal losses. In 1977, my eighteen-year-old nephew, who I loved very much, committed suicide. That same year, I suffered a miscarriage with my first pregnancy. Continued efforts to bear a child proved fruitless. Then, in 1978, when I was twenty-three years old, my gentle, loving father died of lung cancer. There was a brief hiatus from the tragedy. Three months after my father's death, I wound up pregnant and had a healthy baby boy in 1979. Then it was back to the crises. One year later, his father and I divorced and I began a new relationship—this time with an active alcoholic.

My life became insane. Our relationship became violent and I feared losing custody of my son. In the middle of it all, my eighteen-year-old niece was hit and killed by a car. For the next two-and-a-half years I felt as if I was living in hell. I lost my job teaching, a backlash of the insanity at home. When the relationship ended, I was absolutely broken. If I hadn't had my son to care for, I'm sure I would have found a way out of this life.

Instead, I started heavy-duty therapy which gave me a place to sort some things out. There was much that needed sorting. As I was just getting back on my feet emotionally, another alcoholic came into my life. This one had three years of sobriety with the help of Alcoholics Anonymous. I was introduced to a twelve-step program of my own and my life began to change.

Up until then, I thought the world was out to get me. I chose my attitudes and behaviors according to a set of rules based on that perception. My internalized motto was "an eye for an eye," so if you did something I thought was wrong, I was there to punish you somehow. I spent a lot of time thinking of ruining people that I didn't like or disagreed with when I couldn't actively punish them.

When my outer experience did not mesh with my inner expectations, I'd become a shrew. I would whine, complain, push, cajole, lie, withhold, punish, wish destruction upon others and, in general, attempt to manipulate everybody.

I would get angry and throw all of my spouse's clothes out of the front door. Then, two minutes later, I would panic and run outside to retrieve them. My neighbors would stand there and watch me and I would smile and wave as if there was nothing unusual about all of this.

I would try to get you to take my side in every situation where I perceived there was a war between me and anyone else. It didn't take much to constitute a war. As long as you went along with me, my loyalty to you was beyond limitations. I would go to the ends of the Earth to help you and would defend you to the death. Unless, of course, you forgot to show your gratitude the way I thought you should. And woe be to you if, at any time, you did not give me the same loyalty I gave you. Unfortunately, every time I got even with you, you would find a way to retaliate or I would get trampled from some other source. The cycle went on and on.

Now, I don't want you to think that I was this terrible ogre, because I was not. Basically, my heart was in the right place. My perception was off. I simply didn't know I was going about life the hard way; thinking I had to control everything and everybody. I had no focus, no direction. I was not aware that there was a general path I could follow.

I had heard phrases such as "Honesty is the best policy" and I took that to mean it was a nice way to be, when there wasn't a good reason to be dishonest; "Do unto others" meant to go out and fix people who were doing life wrong; "Judge not lest ye be judged" meant I could judge you when I wasn't in danger of being judged for the same thing.

It never occurred to me that Honesty, Generosity and Goodwill were more than just virtuous ways to be. I had no idea that they contained power; not power *over* others, but power to create good in my own life. I came to this new understanding and direction while attempting to recover from the basic mess that I referred to as my life.

HONESTY

One day, while trying to understand the concept of

God, I began toying with the idea that maybe God was Honesty. If so, then nothing bad could ever come out of being Honest,*so long as my Honesty was motivated by kindness.* I had nothing else to lose, so I began practicing honesty to the best of my understanding each day. There were many times when I was terrified of the truth, but I had made a commitment. That meant *risk*—to risk Honesty, even in the face of overwhelming fear and ego problems.

I let my friends know what I was attempting to do and that I was doing it for my emotional health. I stopped gossiping with them. In the process, I began finding Honest friends. I became Honest about my business, about myself and about my family. I learned what I was doing that got me into white lie situations and I changed. I learned to mind my own business by getting Honest with myself about what really was my business.

I thought many times that I would lose my job; instead, I changed to a job I liked better. I thought I would lose friends; my changes were so attractive to many of my friends that they followed suit and I found healthier and more meaningful friendships. I thought I would lose money and be poverty stricken; that has not happened. I discovered that the bank did not want to take my car or my home and that they would do anything to help me get back on my feet. I thought I would lose my good credit and my credibility. Neither of those ever happened. Instead, I found that by keeping in touch with my creditors when times got rough, they considered me trustworthy. Whoa!

People began to show me admiration and trust. They admired my Honesty and knew they could trust me. They would tell me I showed courage. What I showed, was a working faith in a concept, Honesty, that I had come to believe was the essence of God; and I began liking myself—a lot.

GENEROSITY

As time went on, through my practice of Honesty I had acquired many wonderful and healthy relationships. This was fine by itself, but I also noticed that life didn't seem very Generous toward me. I was now doing work that I enjoyed (thanks to Honesty), but it wasn't giving me a sense of security. Money was always an issue and not a comfortable one at that.

I read some books on prosperity that suggested I might be a tightwad if I was always worried about money. In other words, if I felt lacking, I was probably creating my own lack by withholding and being somewhat selfish and greedy. As I walked through my day, I began to notice many areas where I was greedy with time, attitudes and people, as well as money.

I became acutely aware of areas in my life where taking or keeping was much more at the forefront of my mind than giving. And when I was Generous, there was a subtle (if not overt) expectation of some kind of return. I was still somewhat into "an eye for an eye" where it came to giving. Though I had never thought of myself this way, I was beginning to see where I was really quite selfish in nature. I'd always thought I was the giver, the nice guy. But there were always conditions attached to my giving.

I learned that I must risk again, only this time by letting go. Getting Honest was one kind of risking. Now, I was faced with the prospect of letting go of people, places and things that I was hoarding.

Beginning with money, I looked to some teachers for help in getting over this malady of greed and selfishness; teachers who specialized in prosperity issues; ministers, authors, counselors and friends. Through their direction, I was to give Generously, *especially* when I believed I didn't have enough (enough money, time, people, substance).

Waiters/waitresses in restaurants were one source where I could practice. I had a habit of rewarding, punishing or showing off through the tip. My assignment was to leave 15% of the check, no matter what the service was like or who I was with, in order to learn Generosity, without attention to conditions. I've received better service since I started this practice.

I learned to practice Generosity by showing up to social events, classes and meetings. Just by virtue of my commitment and presence, I help the event *be*, and I also experience more of life by doing so.

My car was a greed issue. I would resent picking people up or driving them places unless they offered to help with gas. Now, I offer my services willingly. I wouldn't use the air-conditioning in my car because I was afraid it would use too much gasoline. Now, I stay cool in the heat. I've stopped calculating gas mileage, too.

I had been selfish to myself. I had been selfish with others. By taking a good look at the little things in my day to day life, I have been able to root out a number of things that were blocking my personal progress.

Generosity became illuminated as another facet of God. The result of my generosity is personal freedom from worry. I know I will always have everything I need. I had achieved the sense of security I had been seeking.

GOODWILL

As I generated more life into my daily living, I began to meet others who were doing much more than just surviving securely from day to day. They were creating and living out their dreams. They were busily planning new heights to reach and reaching them. It had never occurred to me to achieve goals I thought were impossible. I asked them what they did, I read lots of books, I listened to tapes, and I took classes.

I tried using affirmations and visualizing my good, but I very quickly became aware of a strong feeling of doubt. The messages I was receiving from my Still Small Voice would say, "You still have some issues to deal with and you know what they are. Just take some time and think about it." After all the good I was putting out into the stream of life, what could possibly have been holding me back?

One more time, I was to be faced with another aspect of myself that I didn't realize was there. It came to my attention one morning while I was reading the newspaper. The headlines featured a story that was distressing to me because it hit close to home. As I read the article, I heard my own mental-action. It was as if I was shouting over a loud speaker. In my head, I had already tried, convicted and executed the guilty party. I thought things like, "He deserves to be killed in the most painful way possible." and "I wish I was the executioner."

It was hard to believe that those thoughts of violence were coming from my head, but they were, clearly and with conviction. I was absolutely furious. My teeth were tightly clenched, I had stopped breathing and my entire perception of life was distorted. Everyone who had irritated me in the past was now at the forefront of my mind. Though they had nothing in the least to do with the newspaper article, I was ready to punish them all.

My Still Small Voice was gently reminding me that I was judging. My first reaction to that was to defend my anger. I believed I had a right to take that kind of mental-action. Justifiable anger, I believe some call it. I heard the justifications start piling up like they did in the past; justifying my dishonesties, justifying my selfishness, justifications that were going to make it healthy for me to hate.

"Any good mother would feel the same way," I retorted to my Still Small Voice. It was then that I heard the words, "Any good mother would *feel*...," and I experienced a sense of understanding. I was doing *more* than feeling; I was cursing and wishing harm. I suddenly realized that *feeling* the sadness for the traumatized victim was different than wishing harm on the individual who, under healthy circumstances, would never have done what he did. He was suffering in a way I could not possibly imagine.

Accomplishing an attitude of Goodwill toward him was more difficult than any practice of Honesty or Generosity. This anger and self-righteous judgment was hidden within my heart. No one knew it existed except me and my blood pressure. Again I had to ask myself what kind of God I believed in. Since my concept of God was Honesty and Generosity, I couldn't imagine hate and harm going along with that.

I realized that any negative judgment was bound to set me on a course of emotional destruction. I had come so far at that point in my growth that I could not see myself quitting now. It was time for a new commitment; an absolute decision to turn *my* thoughts into *God* thoughts and to take a new direction each time I heard myself blaming and wishing harm. This meant taking positive *mental action* at the time it was happening; difficult, but not impossible, and it was absolutely necessary.

I began noticing how much I judged and blamed others in my life. My parents, spouse, family, friends, neighbors, employers and co-workers were all unwilling receptionists of my judgments upon their lives. It was very similar to the way I reacted to those newspaper headlines. Only the circumstances were different.

I made the commitment to practice unconditional Goodwill . To do so I began the regular use of a simple phrase each time I heard myself casting ill-will in any direction: "I wish for your highest Good."

I practiced honing my Goodwill skills by using them while reading the newspaper, watching television, listening to political figures and especially interacting with my family and acquaintances.

As I practiced Goodwill over and over, I began feeling a sense of release, as if something horrible that used to be inside me was gone. There was a peace I had never known, an understanding of life and of situations that made mine much easier to function within. Goodwill was indeed another God power. The feeling it produced was forgiveness, and it did so automatically.

THE UNEXPECTED RETURN—FORGIVENESS

Life became my classroom; relationships and people were the tests. My actions of Honesty and Generosity, and my attitudes of Goodwill could be applied to every person, place and thing, past, present and future, young, middle-aged or older, male or female.

I found that the commitment to practice unconditional Honesty, Generosity and Goodwill toward all, without expectation of payback, was the absolute and simple way to achieve forgiveness, automatically. I wasn't even trying to forgive.

I had spent many years trying to learn how to forgive, and I really gave it my all. I went to therapy and began concentrating on myself instead of others. I did forgiveness affirmations, I wrote or drew the problem on paper and then burned it, I immersed myself in the positives, I practiced saying things such as, "I forgive you," "I release you," "You are free," "Go away!" until I finally came to the conclusion that I was incapable of fully forgiving anyone.

The problem was that I continued to view each person or group of people from the same perspective. Even though I was releasing them, I still could only think of them in a negative light because I was unwilling to see them in any other way. They deserved for me to think negatively about them, I thought.

As I became willing to change my attitude about them and see them from a new angle, I found myself able to release them automatically. One way I do this is by imagining what it is they dream for their life.

If I'm angry at my employer, spouse, friend, etc., I ask myself what I think they would rather be doing right now. What is their dream for their life? My answers have taken me to a deeper dimension of understanding. Instead of seeing them as cold-hearted robots who do nothing but make me miserable, I get in touch with who they really are, what they really want to be doing. Then I do something to invest in their dream. I wish them their highest Good, send them a greeting card or just focus on thinking kindly about them.

It doesn't matter if my conception of their dreams is true. What this method does is to put me in touch with a more loving reality. I begin to see the person from a whole new point of view, and the resentment dissipates. In addition, by changing my negative perception about people in my present, resentments about people in my past seem to disappear automatically. By forgiving in the present, I forgive that which was in the past.

For instance, one day I unexpectedly ran into a person I resented and had never resolved the conflict. Instead of feeling the old resentments, I felt happy to see her. How strange and yet wonderful it felt. I took the opportunity to apologize for my negative attitudes and behaviors with her, cleaning up my side of the past. This was very different for me, indeed.

What I finally realized was that by concentrating on my own Honesty, Generosity and Goodwill toward others, I was automatically treating myself with the same.

THE UNEXPECTED RETURN—SELF-ESTEEM

I was acting, reacting, thinking and feeling in ways that made me appreciate myself. When this happens, things are bound to change, but I didn't realize change was taking place at the time. It wasn't until I heard myself say to myself, "I sure do like the person you are today," that I realized I had actually become a different person than I had been.

This was not a planned affirmation. It just came out.

I was so surprised to hear myself say that to myself that I did a double take. And then, as naturally as the first one, I *re*affirmed what I had just heard myself say. "Yeah! I do. I really do like you a whole lot, Casey. You've worked very hard and have overcome all kinds of fears in order to be a person of Integrity and I like you a lot." My Still Small Voice was shouting in exultation.

I had improved my character and I noticed that I had changed for the better as an individual. That's when the direction of my life began to change.

Up until then, I had conditional good character, relying on other people's behavior or decisions to dictate how I would conduct myself. Now I build unconditional good character, relying only on my commitment to Integrity principles; and the benefits are many.

My environments, my relationships, my jobs, my wardrobe, my facial expressions, my health and even my pets all reflect my new character. Like attracts like. I am attracted to those people and environments that mirror my own character.

THE UNEXPECTED RETURN—AFFIRMATIONS WORK

As I appreciated and respected myself more and more, I saw that my "can't do" attitudes were disappearing. I had removed my pollution. I could see clearly. I realized that there were many things I wanted to do and I knew I would accomplish them all. I began believing that my affirmations and goals were possible and my dreams began coming true. This book and the workshops my spouse and I put on are part of what were once those dreams.

It isn't always easy. I still sink when I attempt to walk on water. But I keep trying. What I have is a healthy paradigm; a guide to help me make the best decisions at any given moment.

There have been many moments of fear since I began living by the principles of Integrity. Getting Honest has meant choosing to move to a town where I loved the climate, giving up the so called security of familiarity and friends. It has meant walking away from a career that offered regular hours, pension plans, three months of vacation and medical benefits. It meant starting a home business with little training and no seed money.

The bills didn't always get paid on time. The mortgage went unpaid for nine months in a row. The business loan (which meant the equipment that kept us *in* business) went unpaid for three months in a row. The only thing that kept us going was our dedication to Integrity.

We stayed in touch with all of our creditors on a regular basis and discovered that none of them wanted to take away our belongings or our home. They did everything possible to help us back on our feet. We accepted the help of the U.S. government through welfare. We went for free food and graciously accepted help from friends when it was offered.

In this process, we suffered from fear, doubt, anger,

humiliation, depression and a multitude of other related challenges. We went for therapy to keep from taking out our anxieties on one another. Throughout this time, we continued to keep the path of our Integrity as clean as possible on a daily basis.

Our personal success was achieved through the method described in this book. One of my fears was that this book would not be taken seriously. I've had fear that the title would confuse people; that no one would want to read it; that my book would never be completed. I've been confused, tired and depressed. I wrote it anyway.

I guess that's what this whole book is really about—doing it anyway—generating action in the most positive direction possible, regardless of the outlying circumstances. You see, I have accomplished a tremendous amount in my life just by putting these principles into action—Honesty, Generosity and Goodwill. There is so much more of life to experience and I'm just getting started.

About the Author

Casey Chaney is a teacher, musician and writer. She currently resides in Beaverton, Oregon with her spouse, Berdell and son, Corey. Also sharing that residence are Springer Spaniel Kila and Mutt Gonzo.

Casey and Berdell give workshops and seminars based on the concepts embodied in this book.

Notes